All Ab

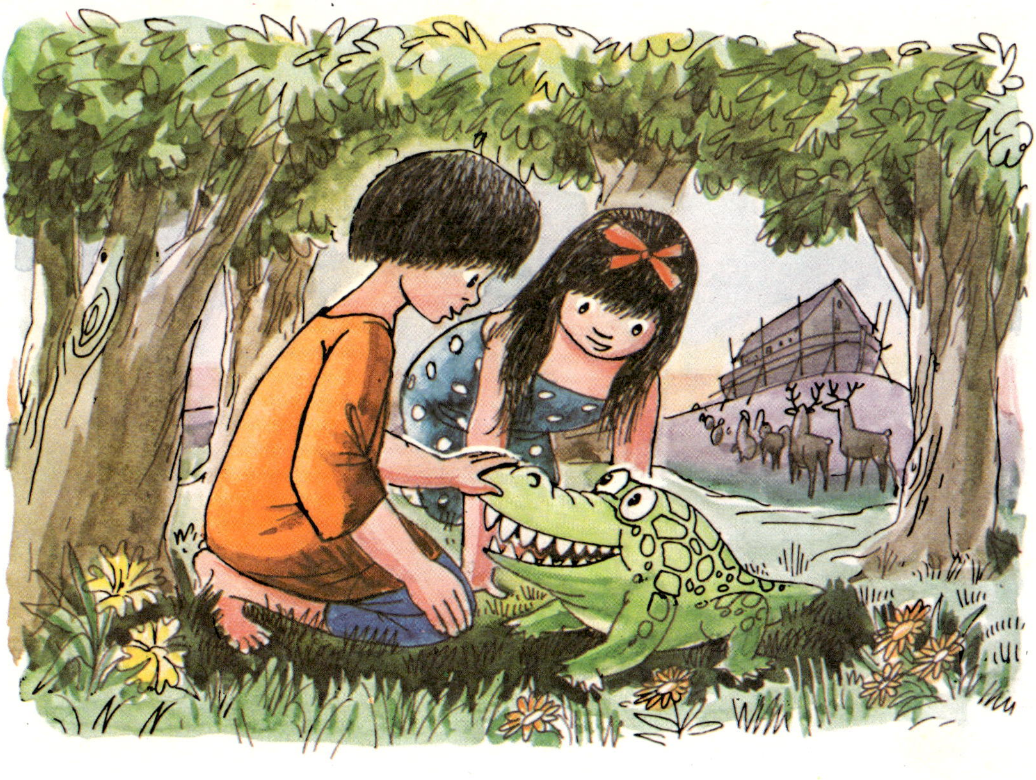

Written and Illustrated by
John Ryan

There was once a boy called Jaffet who was good with animals—

all sorts of different kinds of animals.

He was good with tame ones like dogs, cats, pigs, sheep and cows,

and fierce ones, too.

Even the very big ones didn't frighten him because, in fact,

Jaffet had to look after just about every kind of animal under the sun for his father,

whose name
was Noah.

Noah was building an Ark to put all the animals in when the rain came. For he, and his wife Mrs Noah, knew that it was going to rain

for forty days and forty nights
and that all the world and
everything outside the Ark
would be drowned.

Jaffet had an older brother called Shem who was lean and severe. He had to be, because he looked after the stores and the accounts.

And he had another older brother called Ham who was fat and kind and cheery and did most of the carpentry on the Ark.

Shem's wife was thin, too. She was a good soul, but not very cheerful, whereas Ham had a happy, chubby wife, and her cooking was wonderful.

Jaffet also had a friend called Jannet. She was good with animals too and they both thought that one day they'd probably get married, but that is another story.

This one is about Jaffet's special *animal* friend, who was a baby crocodile called Crockle. Jaffet and Jannet had found Crockle

when they were collecting all the other animals for the Ark. But the trouble was that there were already two perfectly good crocodiles on the list

(or perfectly bad ones), and Jaffet knew that when the time came to go aboard Crockle would have to be left behind,

because Father Noah had said so.

Then one day the whole sky was blotted out with great black clouds, and Noah knew that the time had come.

'Line up the animals, Jaffet,' he cried. 'And remember, Shem, only *one* pair of each kind. That is an order.'

'Just leave it to me, father,' replied Shem. 'I'll see there are no gate-crashers!'

'And don't let me catch you trying to smuggle *that* one aboard,' he said to Jaffet. Poor Jaffet; he knew there was nothing he could do.

So he said goodbye to Crockle and so did Jannet and they both got ready to put all the other animals aboard the Ark.

Crockle crept sadly away, crying a crocodile tear or two.

‘The animals are all in alphabetical order, so the A’s come first,’ called Jaffet, trying to be cheerful. ‘Here’s one pair of aardvarks for a start.’

And one pair of ants.
Wait! I must find my magnifying glass.
Right! Now where are those ants?
Well, they *were* there, but next on the list came the *ant-eaters*!
Hm, maybe alphabetical order wasn't such a good idea! Now we'll have to find some more ants!

Meanwhile, Crockle was wandering along the underside of the Ark.

There he met Ham, who was making sure that everything was watertight and ready for the rain. 'Why, it's young Crockle,' said Ham. 'Look what *I've* just noticed!'

And away went Ham in search of a bung. When he got back there was no sign of Crockle anywhere.

All this while, two by two, the animals were marching into the Ark. It was none too easy getting some of the larger ones through the door and there *was* a certain amount of pushing and shoving,

but for the most part everybody was very well behaved. Last of all came the zebras, and when Shem was satisfied that two of every single kind of animal had gone on board

it was the turn
of the family

and their baggage.

Then, as the sky grew even darker . . .

'Get under cover, everybody,' cried Mr Noah. 'It'll rain before nightfall.'

Later on it was feeding time. 'And remember now, NO ANIMALS MAY EAT ANY OTHER ANIMALS!' said Mr Noah. 'Like it or not, we're vegetarians on this trip!'

So the animals had supper.

There was hay for some,

and fruit for others, and a special tasty porridge

for the fiercer sorts of animal. Everybody enjoyed the meal,

although some found it more difficult than others.

Then the family had their supper.

As it was Mrs Ham's turn to do the cooking it was very good indeed. But Jaffet was too upset to enjoy his food.

He sat down in a corner and thought about Crockle, all alone outside.

Then suddenly he felt something nibbling at his heel.

He looked down, and there was Crockle!

Jaffet was thrilled. 'However did you get *here*?' he said. Just then Ham walked by

and he told Jaffet all about Crockle and the bung-hole. Then they saw Shem,

checking his lists.
'Oh dear,' said Jaffet,
'I'll have to put you back on land, Crockle!'

But Ham said, 'Nonsense! You can't do that.' And he pointed to the latest notice that Noah had put up.

'That settles it, then,' said Jaffet. 'Crockle had best move in with me. No-one will find him there!'

That night the rain began.
Heavier and heavier it fell, but inside the Ark

all the people and the animals
slept warm and snug and dry—

especially Jaffet
and Crockle.